MEDITATIONS FOR YOUTH

MEDITATIONS
FOR YOUTH

Walter L. Cook

ABINGDON PRESS

NEW YORK   NASHVILLE

MEDITATIONS FOR YOUTH
Copyright © MCMLVIII by Abingdon Press

Library of Congress Catalog Card Number: 58-6592

SET UP, PRINTED, AND BOUND BY THE
PARTHENON PRESS, AT NASHVILLE,
TENNESSEE, UNITED STATES OF AMERICA

To my teen-age sons
MERLYN AND BRADFORD

this book is affectionately dedicated

❋

PREFACE

If you are a teen-ager you are probably in a hurry. The two boys in our home always are—except when getting down to breakfast on mornings before school. Urging them out of the house and on their way to school is a major operation for their mother, requiring tact, patience, and plenty of applied psychology.

By 7:30 A.M. the boys are usually through with breakfast and ready to bolt for school. To have a few devotional moments at such a time is a goal not easily achieved.

The following meditations are brief, even for young people in a hurry. I hope you will find them interesting and that they will help make the way of a young Christian a little easier to find. The selections are based upon well-known Bible passages: Exod. 20:1-17 (The Ten Commandments), Ps. 23, Matt. 6:9-13 (The Lord's Prayer), Matt. 25:31-46, and I Cor. 13.

WALTER L. COOK

CONTENTS

OBEDIENCE

EXODUS 20:1-17

And God spoke all these words, saying,

"I am the Lord your God, who brought you out of the land of Egypt, out of the house of bondage.

"You shall have no other gods before me.

"You shall not make yourself a graven image, or any likeness of anything that is in heaven above, or that is in the earth beneath, or that is in the water under the earth; you shall not bow down to them or serve them; for I the Lord your God am a jealous God, visiting the iniquity of the fathers upon the children to the third and the fourth generation of those who hate me, but showing steadfast love to thousands of those who love me and keep my commandments.

"You shall not take the name of the Lord your God in vain; for the Lord will not hold him guiltless who takes his name in vain.

"Remember the sabbath day to keep it holy. Six days you shall labor, and do all your work; but the seventh day is a sabbath to the Lord your God; in it you shall not do any work, you or your son, or your daughter, your manservant, or your maidservant, or your cattle, or the sojourner who is within your gates; for in six days the Lord made heaven and earth, the sea, and all that is in them, and rested the seventh day; therefore the Lord blessed the sabbath day and hallowed it.

"Honor your father and your mother, that your days may be long in the land which the Lord your God gives you.

"You shall not kill.

"You shall not commit adultery.

"You shall not steal.

"You shall not bear false witness against your neighbor.

"You shall not covet your neighbor's house; you shall not covet your neighbor's wife, or his manservant, or his maidservant, or his ox, or his ass, or anything that is your neighbor's."

LIVE IN A BIG WORLD

You shall have no other gods before me.

A high-school senior lived in a large city. After his classes were over he worked for a newspaper company tying bundles of papers for delivery. School work and his part-time job used up most of his time. But every week end he would carry a large telescope to the top of the flat roof of the apartment house where he lived. There at night he studied the stars. His interests were not confined to bundles of newspapers and textbooks on grammar and history. Each week he spent time in a larger world.

Do *you* live in a big world or a small one? If you live in a small world, you may find that your interests are concerned with the size of your weekly allowance, the amount of popularity you enjoy, or a place on your high-school basketball team. It is good to have a fat allowance—if you do not blow it *all* on jukeboxes, movies, and feeds in some "hole-in-the-wall." It is good to be popular. It is rewarding to wear your school letter which shows you are a member of the varsity. Go ahead and make the most of all these things.

But these things can become walls which shut out your view of a larger world. Some of our daily ambitions and achievements can fence in our view. Flashy convertibles, social success, and a fat wad of spending money can become gods to us. If you ask a friend whether he worships "other gods" than the one true God, he will say, "Of course not!" But does he really mean what he says?

It is possible to dwell in a very small world of "things" and fail to make the God of heaven and earth supreme in our daily lives. A person ignores the first commandment when he permits his own small interests to come between him and the stars.

Almighty God, heavenly King, help me to worship thee and no other god. Keep me from permitting selfish interests to block my vision of thy power and greatness. Teach me how to feel at home in a bigger world. AMEN.

GETTING THROUGH TO GOD

You shall not make yourself a graven image.

Suppose that you had never seen a dog in your life. Then one day you were blindfolded and a dog was brought to you to touch—for example, a big collie. First you reached out your hand and touched his tail. What was that? It must be a piece of rope. Then your hand came into contact with his teeth. You said, "These are like little stones kept in a leather pouch." Then you touched his side. This was like the collar on your mother's winter coat.

Even if the collie stood still all the while you were exploring him, you would never know what he really was like. You would not know that he could be a wonderful companion full of friendliness and fun, ready to run with you and come when you whistle. By just touching him you could have no real idea what he is like.

In the second commandment God forbade men to make any graven image. Why? What is wrong with a piece of stone or a piece of wood carved into the likeness of someone? Simply this. Men cannot tell from the outside of a thing what that thing is really like.

We may be sure that when men made the first image of God, they were not trying to do wrong or harm to religion. They were trying in a crude way to make God real so they could be sure of him. Then when they prayed it would not seem as though they were sending their petition into empty air.

The trouble was that soon they found themselves praying to the image itself and worshiping it. They saw the image and forgot almighty God who was represented by that image.

God is a spirit and when we worship him it must be in spirit and in truth. We can admire a mountain or a sunset, but we must not confuse beauty in nature with God himself. He is behind it all, but he is more than, and different from, anyone or anything you can see or touch or hear.

Almighty God, sometimes thou dost seem so far away. Teach me how I may sense thy nearness and feel thy presence in my life. Help me to look often upon Jesus Christ who came to earth to make thee known to all men. AMEN.

IT'S ONLY A HABIT

You shall not take the name of the Lord your God in vain.

"What's wrong with swearing?" Many high-school young people ask this question. Some of them will say, "When I'm mad, sometimes I let go some good, big, sizzling words, but I don't really swear."

The danger is that when you use words dyed a deep, dark, electric blue, you may link some to God's name and then you will be swearing. Then you will be violating the commandment "You shall not take the name of the Lord your God in vain."

Of course there are many kinds of swearing. Some people "get mad" and swear loudly. Others use God's name to punctuate their sentences. These people are just plain lazy; they don't want to bother their heads thinking up adjectives which will help to emphasize what they mean. "Wood swearing" is another kind of profanity. Wood swearing is slamming a door in anger, or kicking a rocking chair or a table leg, and perhaps muttering some words like "Jesus" or "my God."

Many people say, "When I swear I don't mean anything by it—it's only a habit." That's just the trouble. To use the name of God or Christ in a careless, easygoing way is as wrong as to use it in anger.

Think how you feel when you enter a large and beautiful church with beautiful windows and a great organ is being quietly played. Think how you feel when you are standing on a mountain peak that is over ten thousand feet high, and you are looking out over a vast landscape. Think how someone must have felt when he looked for the first time into the Grand Canyon and said, "It seems to be plumb full of hush."

When you lower your voice in a church or get very quiet on a mountaintop, you are feeling a sense of awe. Deep wonder and reverence should fill your soul each time you speak of almighty God. He is your Father and your Creator, and his name must never be repeated except with honor and respect.

Almighty God, so come to me in thy greatness and might that I shall never speak thy name carelessly or in anger. Teach me how best I may reverence thee and always in word and deed bring honor to thy holy name.
AMEN.

FACE TOWARD THE LIGHT

Remember the sabbath day to keep it holy.

Men of science say there are fish which live more than six miles below the ocean's surface. To prove it a Danish scientist rigged a deep-sea trawl off the Philippine Islands and dragged the floor of the ocean. Sure enough he brought some "queer fish" to the surface—mollusks, sea anemones, and sea cucumbers. These creatures of the ocean's bottom had been living where the water pressure is more than seven tons per square inch. They had spent all their lives in cold and darkness.

It is possible for people to live long lives without ever coming up into the light of God's love. That is what Sunday is for. On that day all people should turn away from their jobs and their self-centered pursuits and look toward God who is their maker. There should be a time each week when every person pauses to "remember the sabbath day, to keep it holy."

The sabbath of the ancient Hebrews is not the same as our Sunday, but there are similarities between the two. The Hebrews were commanded to do no work on the sabbath, for this was to be their day of rest. Quite plainly God wished them to make the seventh day different from the other six.

Of course, someone may ask, "Shouldn't we live a holy life *every* day of the week?" Indeed we should. But people may be required to work six days of the week. Although work is blessed by God, once a week people need to make a special effort to worship and rest.

The mayor of a large city proposed that the youthful vandals who were breaking up and defacing monuments in the city parks be compelled to repair them. This was to be the vandal's punishment. The park superintendent wisely commented that men who "tear down" are in no sense worthy to "build up."

Sunday as a day of worship and praise is being torn down. Monuments are reminders of great events and of great lives which have been lived. Sunday should be a reminder of God's love and mercy to men. Let none of us destroy it.

O God, our creator, help me never to forget thy great commandments. Help me faithfully to set aside ample time each week to worship thee and praise thy name. AMEN.

GET ACQUAINTED WITH YOUR PARENTS

Honor your father and your mother.

Just how well do you know your father and mother? It is possible that they are more interesting people than you realize.

Have you ever sat down with your mother and asked her about her early life? Ask her what games she played, what she dreamed she would become, how she liked school, and what her favorite courses were. You might do the same with your father. If you do you may discover that they are real people after all.

You can never know how much your mother wants you to approve of her. She wants you to think that she is pretty special, and when you show that you think she is pretty special, she will be happy all day long. Be enthusiastic about her work, her apple pies, her new draperies, her spring coat.

Once a boy in talking with his mother discovered that when she was a teen-ager she had a great interest in painting pictures. One of her teachers said she had real ability. Then she got married, and in bringing up her children, she had to let her painting interests lapse. One day her son was rummaging about in the attic of their home and he came upon one of the paintings done in her girlhood. He liked it, brought it down to the kitchen, and asked her who was the painter. When she rather shyly admitted that she had painted it years ago, he burst out, "Why, Ma, it's wonderful; you're a real painter." His mother glowed with happiness. And do not think for a moment that your *father* is any different? He'll be thrilled, too, if you appreciate some of his accomplishments.

When you go beyond obedience, and respect, and courtesy, you will be honoring your father and mother. They need your warm responses and appreciation.

Father in heaven, teach me how I may best honor my father and mother. Keep me ever grateful for their care and love for me. May I become, through Jesus Christ, the kind of person they desire me to be. AMEN.

KILLING WITHOUT A GUN

You shall not kill.

You may say, "I'm not going to kill anyone, so this commandment doesn't apply to me." If you are a Christian young person you have probably never been tempted to kill anybody. In the future you will never become an armed thug brandishing a machine gun.

So let's skip this one.

Just a moment; there may be something for you in this commandment, even if you have decided never to become a gun-toting gangster. Although you will never shoot to kill, probably you are aware that sometimes there is hate in your heart. Jesus in his teachings made clear that to hate another person is evil. He said, "You have heard that it was said to the men of old, 'You shall not kill; and whoever kills shall be liable to judgment.' But I say to you that everyone who is angry with his brother shall be liable to judgment." Thus Jesus announced the principle upon which rests the sixth commandment.

"You shall not kill" states the sacredness of human

life. The commandment makes clear that we are to treat the lives of others with respect and reverence.

Right now do you hate anyone? Do you sometimes exclaim about an acquaintance, "How I despise that fellow"? Don't think for a moment that it requires a dead body to make you guilty of killing. Your hate is your murder.

Are you careless of other peoples' lives? Whenever you show indifference to the life of another person you are breaking this commandment. People who are careless of the lives of others might do well to read thoughtfully a sign which was placed on a dangerous highway curve:

Drive slow.

Two fools might meet.

A young fellow who roars down the highway at 85 mph in a snappy convertible with thin tires is not respecting human life—his own or anyone else's. He never knows when a tire will "let go" and send him crashing into another motorist. "You shall not kill" is especially important in these days of souped-up motors and 300-H.P. engines.

In your home, at school, on the highway, at work, almighty God bids us, "Reverence human life."

Father in heaven, who hast created all men in thy image, help me always to respect the rights and lives of others. Keep me from carelessness, indifference, and scorn of all my friends and acquaintances. In the name of Jesus Christ. AMEN.

LOVE IS NO PLAYTHING

You shall not commit adultery.

Years ago in South Africa a man stopped one day to watch several boys who were playing marbles. Every time the boys tossed them, he noticed that the marbles flashed and sparkled in the sunlight. The man wondered why the marbles sparkled so. He asked the boys to let him examine some of the marbles, and to his astonishment he discovered that they were playing with diamonds. It is said that in this way the South African diamond mines were discovered.

Diamonds should be used for something better than a marble game. They can be placed in bracelets, in necklaces, and in engagement rings.

In your teens you are given a great power—the power to make possible the coming of new lives into the world. Later in your life you will fall head over heels in love with some person of the opposite sex. You will want to build a home and share it with this person. Then you will want to use your power to bring a new life into the world. That is why God gave this power to us. He has planned for men and women to reproduce their kind.

This power of yours is something like a diamond. It is precious beyond words. Something that is so valuable must be treated with respect and carefully guarded.

Precious as it is, it may be used for the wrong purpose. God gave the seventh commandment to men and women because he wanted them to use their powers of reproduction in the right way. They must not make a plaything out of love, nor wreck their future lives by surrendering to an unguarded impulse.

In these days it is very difficult to guard the treasure God has given to us. You may feel that to be popular and prove you are a worldly wise and sophisticated person, it is necessary to be "free" in your relations with members of the other sex and sell your purity for a few minutes of excitement.

Boys and girls are bound to find one another attractive, and "dates" are good as well as necessary. But until you are married you must not use the sexual powers which God has given to you. A goodnight kiss is one thing, but a red-hot petting party in a car parked out on some back road is quite another. The former may be harmless enough, the latter may lead to hell. Don't play marbles with diamonds.

Almighty God, who hast created us in thine own image, help me to keep clean in thought and word and deed. Teach me to use the wonderful strength that has been given to me in such a way that I shall never bring injury to others nor harm to my own soul. AMEN.

NOT ALL THIEVES GET LOCKED UP

You shall not steal.

A baffled mother of two little children exclaimed: "My baby sitters used to eat everything in the icebox. Now I have only canned foods in the refrigerator and take the can opener with me when I leave the house."

That's pretty rough!

Some people feel that they aren't stealing unless they take money. Their idea of theft is to be held up by an armed bandit and robbed of fifty dollars. Snitching a grapefruit from a neighbor's icebox, or a fistful of nails from a keg in his shed, without telling him about it, isn't stealing. Or so they say.

People who wouldn't think of robbing a bank will thoughtlessly pick up and carry off little things which do not belong to them. They forget that God's commandment not to steal applies all down the line—to raiding a refrigerator, putting slugs in the jukebox, or "hooking" apples from a farmer's orchard on the way home from school. "You shall have respect for other people's property," is another way of stating this commandment. And there is no difference between stealing a shiny convertible and an armful of kindling wood. The principle is the same.

Articles are not the only things which may be stolen. Time may be stolen too. A fellow who quits work before his part-time job is carried out is a thief. So is the boy who does a careless job cutting the grass on his employer's lawn.

One way to learn to respect the property of others is to study how to get satisfactions from daily living which have little or no connection with *things*. A sunset cannot be stolen. Nothing can rob a mountaintop of its view. Trust in almighty God can belong to all people. No one can steal his hopes and plans for your life. Let God's care loom large in your life. If his love is precious to you, then *things* will come to count for less and less.

Heavenly Father, take from my life the desire to possess that which belongs to someone else. Rather, increase in my heart the wish to put back more into others' lives than I take from them. AMEN.

BILL BLABB'S BIG MOUTH

You shall not bear false witness against your neighbor.

In a certain youth fellowship there are three teen-agers whose names are as follows: Bill Blabb, Lettie Long-Tongue, and Opal Open-Mouth. You can see by their names that their popularity quotient must be tops. They have a reputation for talking too much.

It really isn't the fact that Bill talks so much that makes him a menace. It's a matter of what he and Lettie and Opal say when they do talk. Bill's classmates often say when they hear some gossip being kicked around the school: "That sounds like one of Blabb's stories. There can't be anything in it. Bill just can't tell the truth."

The ninth commandment was written as a warning to the Hebrew people not to give false statements in court about the conduct of other people. But people can lie outside of court and do just as much damage. A high-school junior told a lie about her rival in speech competition, and that lie started a fire of gossip that blackened the reputation of a girl.

A boy was popular in his youth fellowship. The members of the group honored and respected him so much that they elected him president. One boy was bitterly jealous of him, and started to circulate a lie about the new president. Fortunately the other members of the group stopped the story in time to save a reputation.

A writer tells about a mother who happened to pull a loose board off the porch in front of her house and found underneath it twenty-five pieces of costume jewelry which her teen-age daughter had stolen from the local "five and dime."

If your premises were searched, would several damaged reputations be found—damaged by untruthful stories you had told?

There is something we might do that will help us keep this commandment. Crowd out the evil feelings we have for others and make room for good feelings. Think ahead of time of the consequences that will follow the telling of a lie. Do we really want someone's reputation to be splintered and smashed? Maybe you don't like Jane or Sally or June. Do you want their good names to be dragged through the mud? If a name is dragged through the dirt, some of the dirt will stick.

O God of truth, help me to treat others as I myself wish to be treated. Help me to keep my tongue quiet unless I have something good to say about my friends and acquaintances. Help me see the truth, think the truth, and speak the truth all my life. AMEN.

ARE YOU GOOD IN SMALL PARTS?

You shall not covet.

The cast for the school play was being selected. One girl was asked to take a part she thought was beneath her talent. She refused to be responsible for what she contemptuously called a "bit" part. She desired the leading role and was caustic and bitter in her criticism of the girl who got it. Instead of coveting the lead she would have done well to remember what was said of an actor named Charles Butterworth: "Never a great actor he was invaluable in small parts." He did not covet the great roles, but the small ones he got were acted so well that sometimes people remembered *his* performance and forgot the great ones.

In school, at home, in youth fellowship, every young person has some part to play. For instance, the stoker on an ocean liner is as essential as the captain, so he does not need to envy the captain. Without a man to heave coal the vessel would drift at the mercy of wind and wave. The Unknown Soldier may not have carried rows of decorations upon his chest but he has come to have a large place in our hearts. He was invaluable in small roles.

You do not need to envy anyone, for you are different from any other person in the world. With God's help you may bring a kind of goodness and grace into life that no one else can bring. Not another person on this earth can do just what you can do.

O God, as I start out today, make me clean of envy and jealousy. Keep me from being greedy. Help me willingly to accept my tasks at home and in school. May I respect and use the gifts I have, small as they may seem. AMEN.

TRUST

PSALM 23

The Lord is my shepherd, I shall not want;
    he makes me lie down in green pastures.
He leads me beside still waters;
    he restores my soul.
He leads me in paths of righteousness
    for his name's sake.

Even though I walk through the
      valley of the shadow of death,
    I fear no evil;
for thou art with me;
    thy rod and thy staff,
    they comfort me.
Thou preparest a table before me
    in the presence of my enemies;
thou anointest my head with oil,
    my cup overflows.
Surely goodness and mercy shall follow me
    all the days of my life;
and I shall dwell in the house of the Lord for ever.

WHEN YOU ARE BEWILDERED

The Lord is my shepherd; I shall not want.

You've heard the old saying:

> Spring has sprung;
> The grass has riz;
> I wonder where the daisies is.

Spring came to a midwestern college campus, and "Keep Off" signs began to blossom on freshly seeded green lawns. The students paid no more attention to the signs than they did to a waterlogged stick in the frog pond. They continued tramping across the lawns until the local trustees went complaining to the college president.

"Don't blame the students too much," the president said with a grin. "It's a natural thing for people to take short cuts to their destinations. Let's study the route the students take anyway and then build sidewalks the way they are going."

Maybe the college president was right in trusting the

students' sense of direction. But many people are not wise enough to follow the best paths to good goals in life; they need guidance and leadership. The writer of the twenty-third psalm was one person who knew he needed a guide, and in this psalm he spells out how much he appreciates the leadership of almighty God.

When the author of the psalm wished to express an idea of God he called him a shepherd; and a shepherd is one who goes before his sheep and directs their paths.

You have perhaps heard the answer Daniel Boone, the great explorer, made when he was asked whether he had ever been lost. Thoughtfully he said, "No, I never got lost, but I was bewildered once for three days."

The days in which we live are bewildering ones. We are puzzled by the future, and in this atomic age some of us wonder what is going to happen to the world. Let God be your guide.

Some of us find it hard to tell right from wrong. Some of our friends say one thing, others say something else. We are confused. Let God be your leader as he speaks to you through the Bible and through prayer.

Others of us cannot make up our minds what vocation to choose. We wonder whether we shall ever be able to get through school and take our place in a profession or a job where we shall be useful and happy. Here again let God be your guide.

Great God, in this puzzling world help me to see the way that I should go. Keep me from trying to find my way alone in this life. Rather, may I trust in thee as a leader and guide in all that I plan to do. AMEN.

BUILD UP YOUR RESERVES

He makes me lie down in green pastures. He leads me beside still waters.

"People, like boats, toot loudest when they're in a fog." This rare bit of wisdom especially fits the day in which we are living. The world has never been so filled with noise as it is today.

One exhaust on a car isn't enough. "Double-stackers" are now necessary so that the car will leap away from a stop light with a deafening roar. Jet fighter planes taking off from American air bases scream like banshees. Jukeboxes give out with the top tunes, sung at the top of some band leader's lungs. Our password seems to be, "One big noise."

Is it not possible that much of this noise shows how muddled we really are? We don't feel very sure of ourselves. We feel insecure and a little scared of the future, so we turn up the volume. If things are going full blast, the voice of our inner misgivings cannot be heard so easily.

A young man was told by his doctor that he was

incurably ill and that he had but a short time to live. The young fellow went to the Y.M.C.A. in a big city, and said to the clerk at the desk, "Give me an outside room." Afterward he explained to his minister the reason for his request. He said: "Since I was looking into the face of death, I wanted to go somewhere where there was life, and plenty of it. I was afraid of stillness."

How tragic it is that some people must turn to noise and strong action when life backs them into a corner. How tragic it is that some of us do not have inner reserves upon which we may depend when we are in trouble.

When we turn to God in the midst of our problems, he does not give us his help accompanied by a brass band. He helps us as we lift up our eyes unto the hills, or as we permit him to lead us "beside still waters."

The next time you feel overwhelmed by discouragement, seek out some quiet place and give God a chance to speak to you. David, who wrote the twenty-third psalm, was a man of action if ever there was one. He was a mighty leader, yet he was wise enough to follow the guidance of the Lord who led him into paths of quietness where his spirit could be refreshed and strengthened.

O God, our Father, I thank thee that I can depend upon thee; that thou dost care about me in the midst of my problems and perplexities. Help me to trust in thee for strength and help in every time of need. AMEN.

BUILDING UP YOUR EYESIGHT

He restores my soul.

An American jeweler went to Antwerp to buy diamonds. A dealer brought out a large tray of the gems, so that the American might inspect them. After looking at several the jeweler turned his eyes away from the tray. He did this often while making his selections. "Why did you look away from the diamonds from time to time?" asked the dealer. The jeweler replied: "As I gazed upon the stones, the keen edge of my vision was dulled. When I looked away for a moment, that keenness returned."

Every young Christian who knows almost by heart many of the stories of the Bible has in his memory a collection of precious jewels. The Lord's Prayer is surely a gem of helpfulness. Have we gotten so used to hearing and "saying" this greatest of all prayers that we no longer discern the wonder and greatness of it? We have read so often the story of the good Samaritan and the prodigal son that these jewels no longer seem to shine with the luster they once had.

How shall our hearing be restored, how shall we build up our eyesight so that we may see in these things the wonder of God's love? There are many ways.

You might look away toward some great mountain. A glance at its soaring greatness may renew your knowledge of God's strength. Look at the mirrored surface of a lake in the early morning. In its calmness you will be reminded of God's peace which passeth understanding. Sometimes turn away from your schoolwork and social interests to the quietness of your own church. Go when no one is there. Stand in the auditorium and feel the overarching greatness of God.

After seeing the majesty of a mountain and catching the quietness of a lake, and feeling the hush of the great room of your church, turn once again to the jewels of Scripture.

O God, keep me from "getting used" to the wonderful truths of my faith. Give to me the seeing eye and hearing ear that I may discern the beauty of thy Word. When I seem far away from thee, help me to turn to thee, the one who can restore my soul. AMEN.

NEEDED: FOLLOWERS AS WELL AS LEADERS

He leads me in paths of righteousness.

When a high-school senior applied for admission to a well-known college, a questionnaire was sent to her father. While working on the questions her dad came to this one: "Is she a leader?" He thought a moment and then wrote: "I am not sure she is a leader, but I know she is an excellent follower."

A few weeks later he received this letter from the dean of the college. "As our freshman group next fall is to contain several hundred leaders, we congratulate ourselves that your daughter will also be a member of the class. We shall be certain of one good follower." Apparently all the other fathers claimed that their daughters were good leaders.

So many people think they must be leaders, and indeed every group needs committee chairmen. But people are needed who will work with chairmen. Not everybody can be a leader, so more people should study how to be good followers.

If you are going to be a follower you must set about choosing the right leader. Some leaders will take you down a dead-end street or conduct you up a blind alley. This century has witnessed leaders like Hitler, Mussolini, and Stalin, whose fondest desire seemed to be to push other men over the brink of disaster. It is of supreme importance that all of us follow a leader who will guide us into paths of righteousness.

How did the farmer of fifty years ago plow his furrow straight on a hillside? Surely he accomplished it by keeping his eyes on a fixed point at the opposite end of the field until he reached it. How may a Christian live a "straight" life today in the midst of so many influences which seek to lead into paths of unrighteousness?

The Good Shepherd is the one upon whom we must keep our eyes. When we are pulled or pushed by some self-appointed leader of the crowd toward impurity and dishonesty, let us ask God to help us surrender our wills to Christ.

Almighty God, I thank thee that thou hast made thyself known in Jesus Christ. Help me to follow his guidance wherever he leads. Keep me loyal, faithful, and true to the Good Shepherd all the days of my life. AMEN.

WHEN LIFE TAKES A SWING AT YOU

Even though I walk through the valley of the shadow of death, I fear no evil; for thou art with me.

Does your boat have a captain? Does your plane have a pilot? Does your car have a driver? Does your life have a guide?

Every person needs a guide. There are times when we feel pretty adequate. The days go along like a song. Then all at once something goes wrong. The boat begins to rock. The car begins to swerve and skid, and we see plenty of trouble ahead. Life doesn't turn out to be so simple as we had thought it was.

Sometimes the parents of teen-agers act as though their son's or their daughter's troubles didn't add up to a hill of beans. Dad thinks *his* difficulties are real, but he seems to think that yours are practically nonexistent. You know better.

It is no small disappointment when you plug hard, really plug, to pass a math exam and then flunk it cold. When you feel yourself dropping behind in your class, it hits you where it hurts. It is no small matter to put all you have into a fight to make the team. Everybody needs a bit of recognition; you had hoped to get yours by being a valuable member of a baseball club. Then you had to sit it out on the bench all year.

Then there comes times when life swings a real haymaker. Perhaps you lose your best friend, or you get hurt and have to be "holed up" in a hospital room for two weeks. The writer of this psalm knew a good deal about the rough places of life. The phrase, "Even though I walk through the valley of the shadow of death," may be translated, "Even though I walk through the valley of dark shadows, I fear no evil, for thou are with me."

When life gets rough we do need someone with us. And God has promised to be our companion. Our troubles *are* real, but God's friendship is real too. A young man who was deep in trouble found God and described his experience this way: "Before I met him I was looking down; after I met him I was looking up."

O God, deepen my trust in thee, so that when discouragements and disappointments come my way I shall know that I am not alone. May I live so near to thee every day that I shall not be fearful to walk through valleys of dark shadows. AMEN.

WHEN YOU GET CRITICIZED

Thou preparest a table before me in the presence of my enemies.

Do you have enemies? Sometimes you are sure you have them. Probably there is no one who would push you out of a ten-story window or shove you in front of a speeding automobile. Just the same, you are rather sure that you have at least a couple of acquaintances who would like to "do you dirt."

For example, you feel that people who criticize you are your enemies. You are sure you have critics. They say spiteful things behind your back. They point out your blunders even to your face, and sometimes they do this in front of your friends. Surely such people are your "enemies."

Well, how do you take the criticism of these enemies? The next time somebody gives a poor estimate of your character, ability, or personality, stop and think whether there is any truth in the words which are said about you. If there is some truth in the statements, hurry out of your house, run over to your critic's home, ring his doorbell, and warmly thank him for his words. After all, if you are ever going to improve in character and personality, you need to be coached a little. Criticism can be considered as coaching. And remember sticks and stones are thrown only at fruit-bearing trees.

But there is a different kind of enemy-critic you may have. He is one who criticizes you unjustly. Maybe he tells stories about you which are untrue. Surely he is a bad enemy to have, and you are afraid of him, or at least angry with him.

The writer of the twenty-third psalm has a word for you. He states that even when he is surrounded by enemies God cares for him and protects him. He says with quiet confidence, "Thou preparest a table before me in the presence of my enemies."

If God stands by us even when we are surrounded by enemies, then there are no hopeless problems, but only people who have grown hopeless about them. When unjust critics seem to be having a field day at your expense God is nearby (setting the table of his goodness for you). If some people seem to be determined to do us harm, the Good Shepherd is equally determined to be with us and to help us.

O God, I thank thee that when the going is hardest thou art with me. I do not ask thee to make all my burdens light, but to give me strength to bear them. In the name of the Good Shepherd. AMEN.

GOODNESS THAT SPILLS OVER

Thou anointest my head with oil, my cup overflows.

A complaint was made to the service department of a telephone company. It was in the form of an unusual request from an old lady. "My telephone cord is much too long," she said. "Would you please pull it back from your end."

God never pulls anything back from his end. He gives and gives and gives until our lives are filled with his blessings. The psalmist knew about God's abundant giving, and he put it this way: "My cup overflows."

It was the daily task of a shepherd to defend his sheep when they were in peril. His job was to fight off robbers and beasts of prey. But a good shepherd performed services for his flock which were over and above his regular duties. There was something "extra" in the services he rendered. For one thing, a shepherd would often find that his sheep had suffered minor head wounds from thorn bushes, or bruises from sharp stones, and he would anoint these wounds with oil. Undoubtedly the sheep would recover from these wounds, but the use of healing oil would bring them comfort.

God treats us in the same lavish manner. He might have placed a dozen stars in the sky; instead he spangled the whole canopy of heaven with them, adding beauty to the night. He might have given us one bird's song; instead he gave us the songs of many birds, so that a spring morning is often turned into a beautiful concert.

He also gives to us his love and care, and he has made possible deep friendships which endure for a lifetime. As a crowning gift he sent his only begotten Son to us. In Jesus Christ he gave us the perfect reflection of himself. That was his supreme present to us.

It is a crying shame that we have come to take God's overflowing goodness for granted. Think of one example. There was a time many centuries ago when people were forbidden even to own a Bible. Right now you probably have one on a stand near your bed. You own it and can read it any time you wish. This privilege is an expression of God's overflowing love to you.

Our Father in heaven, we thank thee that thou hast given us so much more than we can ever deserve. Help us daily to give of our love and devotion to thee. AMEN.

ARE YOU FACING IN THE RIGHT DIRECTION?

Surely goodness and mercy shall follow me all the days of my life; and I shall dwell in the house of the Lord for ever.

The principal of a boy's school was a sincere Christian and had been a fine friend to many young people. One day he was taken suddenly ill and his doctor told him that he was dying. The principal sent a message to his students. He said, "Tell the young men I've grown surer of God every year of my life, and I've never been so sure now that I'm about to die."

There are at least two important things about the journey of life: the trip itself and the destination. The principal said that he had been sure of God on the journey and that he was sure of him as he was reaching his destination. You will notice that the psalm writer speaks of goodness and mercy following him all the days of his life, and then he speaks of dwelling in God's house forever. He is saying that God's care and love are for every day of life, but that it is also available at the end of this life and "forever."

The business of dying seems a long way off—as indeed it is for most young people. Two teen-agers who were talking about death make this point clear. One of them said he didn't like to think about death very often—it made him uncomfortable. The other boy said, "I don't mind thinking about it. I'm only sixteen. I'm not going to die for at least fifty years. Look at all the time I've got."

Therefore the first thing a young person should think about is not so much his destination as the journey of life itself. If you live close to God now, you will need have no fears when you are old. If God gives you daily of his love and mercy, then you may be sure of his blessing forever.

No one should live as though he were a survivor in a leaky lifeboat. Such a person lives in constant dread. Rather, he should learn to depend upon God's goodness and mercy.

A fisherman with his limit of brook trout left the stream where he had been fishing and started through the woods toward home. On his way he crossed a large open field filled with daisies and noticed that the flowers were all facing in the same direction. The heart of each flower was turned toward the sun.

The goodness and mercy of God are ever yours if you will keep your heart turned toward him. When the sun sinks out of sight and the day is over, God will still be with you.

O God of love, I am thankful to thee that thou hast promised to be my everyday companion. Make me always aware of thy great mercy which will help to keep me from loneliness, fear, and worry. AMEN.

PRAYER

MATTHEW 6:9-13

Pray then like this:
    "Our Father who art in heaven,
    Hallowed be thy name.
    Thy kingdom come,
    Thy will be done,
      On earth as it is in heaven.
    Give us this day our daily bread;
    And forgive us our debts,
      As we also have forgiven our debtors;
    And lead us not into temptation,
      But deliver us from evil."
    For thine is the kingdom, and the power,
    And the glory, for ever. Amen.[1]

---

[1] This last phrase is from the King James Version of the Bible. It does not appear in the Revised Standard Version.

WHAT'S IN A NAME?

Our Father who art in heaven, hallowed be thy name.

A mother of five boys did not want any of them to be nicknamed. So she named the first one William, knowing full well that for a time he would be called Billie or Willie or just plain Bill. But she used a device in naming the remainder of her sons which she believed would prevent any of them from being nicknamed.

After William she named them Wilmot, Wilbur, Wilfred, and Willis. Then she sat back thinking that people would have to call her sons by their real names.

She was wrong, for her sons' friends called them Chuck, Skinny, Tubby, and Buddy.

Sometimes the names we give to our friends suggest something about the persons named. Size and shape may be indicated by the nicknames Tubby, Skinny, or Slim.

When we address God in the Lord's Prayer, we say, "Our Father." This is how Jesus addressed God. Jesus could have called him Emperor, King, and Judge, for in

61

a way God is all these. Instead he chose a term which brought God close to the needs of all people.

In Jesus' day "father" was head of the household, ruler of family life, and the final arbiter of everything that took place in the lives of his children. On Jesus' lips no other name of God is heard so often as Father.

As we have seen, names may have meaning in themselves. For Jesus the term father suggested power, justice, the right to command, and, above all, love. So we may know that when we pray "Our Father," we are speaking to one who will redirect our paths when we have lost our sense of direction in our daily living. We are talking to one who still cares for us when we do wrong, and who will help us when we try to do right.

God our Father cares for us whether our conduct is good or bad, just as a loving earthly father loves his sons whether they obey him or defy him. If yesterday you did that which was evil and ignored his commands, he still invites you to repent and to make a new beginning.

If today you feel you may be tempted in some way to disobey God, speak to him right now in your heart, and he will strengthen your will and guide your steps.

WHAT'S IN A NAME?

O God, we are thankful that we may think of thee as our Father. We are glad that we are loved and cared for beyond our deserving. Keep us in thy way this day, and bring us to a fuller knowledge of thy will for us. AMEN.

WHO IS YOUR BOSS?

Thy kingdom come, thy will be done.

A couple of boys in junior-high school built a club-house in a yard between their homes. On one of the walls, in letters not too evenly printed, was a list of club rules. The first rule read: "Nobody act big, nobody act small, everybody act medium."

Perhaps you say, "Good, they had the right idea; there wouldn't be any snobs in that club. Everybody would be equal." To have equality in a society of friends does have its advantages, but equality can be carried too far. There is a tendency among some people to refuse to admit that there is *anybody* over them —even God.

You will notice that Jesus' prayer includes the words "thy kingdom come." If you are a subject in a kingdom, then indeed you do have someone "over" you. Then you recognize the authority of a sovereign to whom you owe obedience.

Once you have acknowledged that God is your sovereign, the second part of the phrase follows naturally—

"thy will be done." When you welcome God as your king, you permit him to direct your paths and guide your footsteps. But sometimes this is hard to do. We want to be complete "boss" of our own lives.

Ask yourself these questions: "Do I permit God always to guide me in my relations with people of the opposite sex?" "Is God my sovereign when I am given a chance to pass on a poisonous story about someone I don't like at all?" "Is God my King when the gang starts telling smutty stories, or to show I'm a great guy do I join in and laugh loudest of all?"

Jesus permitted God to be the sovereign of his whole life, but even Jesus needed to pray in the Garden of Gethsemane, "Not my will, but thine be done." In your athletic clubs, in your home, and in the social whirl, be sure that God is your king. Every day seek to do his will.

Almighty Father, we acknowledge thee as our king. Teach us how to bring our wills wholly under thy control in our daily living. May we, through thought, word, and deed, bring glory to thy holy name. AMEN.

GOD CARES ABOUT YOU

Give us this day our daily bread.

An American girl once asked a famous French author why he didn't visit the United States. He replied that he hesitated to visit a country where he could not speak the language. "You see," he said, "I know only two sentences in English: 'Please give me a hamburger'; and 'I want a hot dog.' "

"Oh," said the girl, "with a vocabulary like that you could take a trip clear across the country."

Food is mighty important. When you dash into the kitchen after school you are hungry enough to eat anything. Perhaps only a person who has tried to stay alive for days with no food can fully appreciate this request. But at some time in almost all our lives we have known what it is to be ravenously hungry.

In the day when Jesus taught this prayer to his disciples there was a great deal of hunger. In his time there were very few dinner tables which groaned under the weight of tempting dishes. Today we take good food so much for granted that many people do not bother even to pause long enough to say "thank you" to God before they begin the big gulp.

When Jesus included this phrase in his model prayer, he showed quite plainly that God is interested in the physical needs of people. He cares that they have clothes on their backs and roofs over their heads.

Add to this: God cares for those who are physically handicapped. When we are lame, or hard of hearing, or have poor eyesight, God cares.

How can we know this? We can be sure of it because Jesus the Son of God showed such concern for the broken bodies of men. Everywhere he went he touched them, healed them, and blessed them. It is wonderful to know that God is interested in helping us be decently clothed and fed. He will help us meet our day-by-day needs.

Our Father in heaven, we thank thee for thy care for us. Keep us from relying upon thee to do for us what we may do for ourselves. May we do our share in keeping strong and well in mind and body. AMEN.

THE TRICK OF GETTING EVEN

And forgive us our debts, as we also have forgiven our debtors.

When her boy friend quit dating her, a girl in Boston, Massachusetts, slashed the tires on his car, threw sand into the gasoline tank, and let out all the antifreeze in his radiator.

Not all disappointed people go to such a length to "get even" with those who have wronged them. Some people just simmer and stew and carry a grudge after they have been hurt.

Jesus calls upon us to ask God to help us forgive others. Unless we do forgive those who hurt us we shall not be the kind of people whom God himself will forgive. In other words, our own forgiveness from God is based upon our willingness to forgive those who do us wrong.

Once a high-school boy owned an expensive fishing pole which he loaned to a friend. When the friend used it, he was careless with the borrowed property. Beside a brook he jabbed it into alder clumps, dropped it into the water, and slammed it against rocks. Result—the pole was ruined.

The owner felt he got a raw real—as in truth he did. He said: "I treat everyone fairly who treats me that way, but if a guy takes my hide, I'll skin him back first chance I get." That's the kind of talk we understand.

But Christ calls upon us to rise above the attitude of "I'll give him back just what he sent." He calls upon us to forgive. And when we genuinely and honestly do forgive, we may help to change for the good the person who did us dirt. That's the grandest way in the world to get "even." For if we do not forgive others their trespasses against us we shall try to "square accounts." When we do that, we shall take our part in a vicious circle of hate and dislike. *Someone* must forgive and break the circle of bad spirit. The person who does break it is the kind of person who will be forgiven by God.

O God, help me to put myself in the other person's place to see how he thinks and feels. Give me a greater understanding of people who fail me. And even when I cannot fully understand the motives of others, still give me the grace to forgive. AMEN.

WHEN TEMPTATION HITS HARDEST

And lead us not into temptation.

One Sunday morning a boy left his home and started across a field carrying his telescope fishing pole. His dad sighted him, stuck his head out a window, and called to him.

"Hey, Son, I thought I told you not to go fishing on Sunday mornings."

"I'm not planning to do any fishing," came the boy's answer.

"Then what are you doing with that fishing rod?"

"Well, I thought I'd just take it along in case I got tempted."

Some people run away from temptation while others sort of crawl away from it, hoping it may catch up with them.

This phrase in the Lord's Prayer, "lead us not into temptation," is a hard one to understand. Surely it applies to the person who wishes to successfully avoid giving in to temptation, not to the person who would really like to give in.

Perhaps the expression is best explained as a sort of cry of a heart to God from someone who has found that resisting temptaton is very hard. "O God, when I am weak and uncertain of my own moral strength, keep me from temptation," may well be the meaning.

Any rotten old log can float downstream, but it takes a firm hand to steer a boat upstream against a strong current. When the gang is going along in the right direction, you have little difficulty keeping faith with Christ; but when the crowd heads for mischief, then you have your troubles steering your course according to the highest and best you know.

Temptation always seems to come along when we are weakest. Perhaps with Christ's help you have been victorious over some sinful impulse. Overcoming that one temptation leaves you too "beaten up" to face another one. At such a time you might cry out to God, "I can't hold out if I am tested again; spare me, and do not let me be tempted."

Our kind Father in heaven, who dost understand us and all our weaknesses, teach us well how to lean upon thy great power. Show us how to draw upon thy strength when we are tempted. Keep us ever in a mood to resist all evil impulse and desire. AMEN.

HOW BIG IS YOUR MUSCLE?

Deliver us from evil.

How strong are you? Perhaps you can swim a mile and a half across a lake and afterward not have an aching muscle.

Perhaps you can play three sets of tennis and still feel as fresh as a daisy.

Possibly you can work ten hours at one end of a crosscut saw and after dinner spend the evening playing seven innings of softball.

How strong are you when it comes to doing the hard right? Do you need to pray often the prayer of a teen-ager: "O Lord, prop me up in all my leaning places." This young fellow knew he wasn't strong in some ways.

Maybe you are a person who knows only too well that he is not strong enough to win out over a bad habit or to conquer some temptation. At such a time you may pray, "Deliver me from evil." If you ask God to help you it is not a sign that you are a moral weakling. There are some battles in life which we simply cannot win without the help of God. All of us need a Saviour to do for us what we cannot do for ourselves.

Some people feel that they can stand for high principles without benefit of outside help. They feel that they can walk on thin ice without breaking through, that they can play with fire without getting burned. Other people are not so sure of themselves and their own will power. These words from the Lord's Prayer are for them.

Other people feel pretty independent. They say, "I would be ashamed to ask God to do for me what I should do for myself." Maybe such people have to tumble into some ditch before they learn that they must depend upon a guide. It takes a humble person to admit that he cannot always find his way alone. Only a humble person will pray, "Deliver me from evil."

Apply these words to the hours which lie ahead of you. "O God, deliver me from impurity and unclean thoughts." "Deliver me from dishonesty at examination time." "Deliver me from speaking hot and angry words when my mother and father feel they must punish me." "Deliver me from unfair criticism of my teachers from whom I always expect justice."

O God, teach us to rely more and more upon thee. We do not ask thy help because we have earned it, but because we need it so. In thy great mercy guide us this day, keep us from harm, and deliver us from evil. AMEN.

IS THE WORLD GOING TO SMASH?

*For thine is the kingdom, and the power, and the glory,
for ever.*

Keith and Brad were talking about a TV drama they
had both been watching. After the program was over
Keith said, "That was a swell show." But Brad said,
"I liked it too, only there was one thing wrong with
it—it had a sad ending."

Almost everybody likes a story with a happy
ending. The authors of novels and short stories often
drag the reader through all kinds of harrowing ex-
periences which seemingly can end only in tragedy.
Yet skillful writers often wind up by giving the plot
a twist that results in a happy ending.

Strangely enough the story of Jesus' life is really a
tragedy with a happy ending. Christ was beaten and
scorned and tortured and finally crucified. Surely, you
say, his work resulted in tragedy. But did it? Do not
forget his resurrection.

God sent Jesus into the world so that men would be
saved from their evil ways. Jesus taught and healed

and blessed, and for all his pains—a cross. But in three days God raised him up.

Some days when you read the newspaper you get the idea that the devil is captain of the winning team and that God's plans are doomed to failure. We feel like the father whose little son was asked by the teacher in social studies, "What is the shape of the world?" And the boy said quickly, "My father says it's in the worst shape he ever knew it to be."

The world was bad enough in Jesus' day, but he had faith in God, and the prayer concludes with his vote of confidence in his heavenly Father: "For thine is the kingdom, and the power, and the glory, for ever."

Perhaps in this atomic age you wonder what the future holds for you, and you are fearful that the world is going to go to smash and you along with it. It seems as though everything nailed down is coming loose. When you feel that way repeat softly to yourself the last words of the Lord's Prayer.

We praise thee, O God, that all things in heaven and in earth are under thy dominion. Keep us from becoming fainthearted and faithless, even when right seems to be crucified and wrong seems to be enthroned. AMEN.

SERVICE

MATTHEW 25:31-40

When the Son of man comes in his glory, and all the angels with him, then he will sit on his glorious throne. Before him will be gathered all the nations, and he will separate them one from another as a shepherd separates the sheep from the goats, and he will place the sheep at his right hand, but the goats at the left. Then the King will say to those at his right hand, "Come, O blessed of my Father, inherit the kingdom prepared for you from the foundation of the world; for I was hungry and you gave me food, I was thirsty and you gave me drink, I was a stranger and you welcomed me, I was naked and you clothed me, I was sick and you visited me, I was in prison and you came to me." Then the righteous will answer him, "Lord, when did we see thee hungry and feed thee, or thirsty and give thee drink? And when did we see thee a stranger and welcome thee, or naked and clothe thee? And when did we see thee sick or in prison and visit thee?" And the King will answer them, "Truly, I say to you, as you did it to one of the least of these my brethren, you did it to me."

❈

LOST IN A BLUR

I was hungry and you gave me food.

One morning a clever young man showed up at high school saying that he had a new invention he was going to put on the market. He was sure it would mean a fortune to him.

"What is it this time?" his friends wanted to know.

"It's an extra key for a typewriter. When you don't know how to spell a word, you hit that key and it makes a blur that might be an *a*, an *i*, or a *w*, or almost anything else you want."

To some of us religion is a sort of blur too. We go to youth fellowship meetings, we attend morning worship almost every Sunday of the year, and we get a good warm feeling when the choir sings a pretty anthem. Oh, it's all very vague!

But our Christian duties are really not vague at all. In the teachings of Jesus our duties toward God and our obligations to other people are plainly defined.

In the story of the last judgment (Matt. 25:31-46), Jesus outlines the way in which his followers should treat their fellow human beings. The things he tells us to do are as clear as mountain peaks on a sunny day. He calls upon us to render service to people who are hungry or lonely or in prison.

Look around you. Can you think of a single person who is really hungry? The members of your algebra class and basketball team look very well fed. All your friends seem to have what they need to eat: good cuts of beef, ice cream, plenty of bread and milk. Where can a hungry person be found?

Well, don't be too "local" about the matter. Use a little imagination. When you put a gift into the missionary side of your offering envelope, a fraction of that coin will be going to someone in the world who needs food. Granted, you don't put in much. Your allowance hardly keeps you in chewing gum, movies, and sodas. But give all you can, because when you do you are making a gift to Christ himself.

O God, help me to see beyond the boundaries of my own circle of acquaintances to the needs of people in other lands. Touch my heart, that I may ever be willing to give generously to those who are less fortunate than I. Make me ever mindful that as I give to those in need I am giving also to thee. AMEN.

ATTENDING TO TRIFLES

I was thirsty and you gave me drink.

Do you know that one small boy can break up a band concert? He can do it—by sucking a lemon in front of the players. Think of it, trumpets, tubas, trombones, and French horns—all kinds of instruments except drums and cymbals—falling silent before a boy with a lemon.

Many times it's the little things which count against us and put our Christian living out of commission. Often we overlook little kindnesses we should be performing for others. Frequently we forget to speak the word of appreciation to some member of our family who needs encouragement.

Jesus once underscored the importance of giving a cup of cold water to a thirsty child. Such a kindness seems too small to even mention. Our Lord is really making clear that no kindness is too small to be noticed by God.

Are you quick to give to your acquaintances the little attentions they sometimes need? Probably you

are alert to render service to someone who is in dire
straits. You would be the first to provide a steak dinner for a starving man. If an automobile piled up against
a stone bridge near your house, you would rush to the
scene to offer what aid you could. In another person's
crisis you would rush to his aid with all the speed you
could muster.

But do the little inconspicuous needs of people af-
fect you? This is where many of us fail—we do not
attend to trifles—or what seem to us to be trifles.

How about a word of encouragement to your mother
who washes and mends and cooks and irons. Do you
ever let her know you are grateful for her helpful care?

How about the classmate of yours who is caught in
a desert of discouragement. Only yesterday he flunked
a crucial examination, after really studying hard for
it. A word of quiet understanding about now might
bolster his faltering faith in himself. A little thing? To
be sure. But daily living is made up of little things.

*O eternal God, to whom every one of us is important,
never let me forget that I owe kindness and helpfulness
to all whom I know. May no deed of kindness seem so
small to me that I will neglect to perform it.* AMEN.

HAVE YOU EVER BEEN LONELY?

I was a stranger and you welcomed me.

Have you ever been lonely?
Have you ever been blue? *

This question, which comes from a once popular song, could be answered "yes" by many of us. Almost all of us have been lonely at some time in our lives.

A young man decided to study for the ministry and enrolled in a divinity school. For a year, after he entered the school, he lived in a dormitory with forty-five other men. At the end of the year he quit. Why?

Perhaps the reason for his leaving after one year can best be explained by a note he wrote to the dean of the theological school, after he decided not to return. "Dear Mr. Dean," he wrote, "I am not coming back to school this fall. I have always wanted to become a minister, but a minister must know how to get along with all sorts of people. In this I failed. I did not get along at all with the other men in the dorm. I was never so lonely in my life!"

Think of that. He had a roommate. He ate in a dining hall with other men. He studied in the library with classmates. He even played basketball in the gym with many of the fellows. And yet these were his very words: "I was never so lonely in my life."

Look around you for a moment. In your homeroom at school there may be some boy who feels that he "just doesn't fit." Have you ever gone out of your way to "pass the time of day" with him?

In your youth fellowship there may be a girl who is trying to be one of your group. She may be trying harder than you think. But she always feels as though she were a stranger. She may want with all her heart to feel that she *belongs*. With a great longing she is reaching out, hoping that someone will respond to her.

Loneliness is an aching empty feeling. Jesus himself knew about loneliness—on a hillside praying, in the Garden of Gethsemane, on the cross, he must have known the bitterness of being all alone.

Open your eyes today. Try to understand how others feel. Then see what you can do by a gesture, a word, or a glance, that will help a lonely person to feel your comradeship.

O God, our friend and helper, teach me to feel a little the hurts of others. Show me how to bring quiet companionship to someone who may be hungry for friendship. Help me to say just the right thing to a person who needs a companion. AMEN.

INVESTING YOURSELF IN THE BEST

I was naked and you clothed me.

Centuries ago a farmer worked for seventeen years to learn to balance a shepherd's crook on his chin. At last he mastered the trick and called all his neighbors and friends together so they might watch him perform his great act.

Put this bit of foolishness alongside the history of distinguished men who have struggled all their days to accomplish some great purpose which would be a blessing to mankind. There have been dedicated men and women who have done all in their power to bring an end to the poverty, hunger, and disease in the world.

It is possible to fool away a great talent on minor matters. You can become a famous collector of match covers. (One young fellow recently boasted that he had accumulated fifteen thousand of these and had strung them on wires in his den.) You may become the best jew's-harp soloist in all Christendom. You may practice until you can stand on one foot for two hours. So what?

Why not give your interest, your skill, yourself, to some great cause. Jesus speaks of many such causes in this chapter of the Bible. He said plainly that feeding the hungry, visiting the sick, and providing clothes for the poor, are important. In fact, this work is so essential that those who rendered such service would receive a great blessing, while those who failed to care for the needs of others would be punished.

"Well," you say, "there isn't anybody around here who really needs clothes to wear."

Perhaps not long ago the president of your youth fellowship said that the group had been invited to contribute articles of clothing for a mission station in South America. A box was being packed by your church to be sent to the needy. You didn't pay too much attention at the time. It seemed a small matter. And yet there are the words of Christ, "Truly, I say to you, as you did it to one of the least of these my brethren, you did it to me."

Almighty God, keep me from wasting my time and effort on minor matters. Teach me how I can invest my time in the best way. May my whole life be lived in such a way that I shall bring glory to thy holy name. AMEN.

YOU'RE THE DOCTOR

I was sick and you visited me.

What happens to you when you come home saying that your throat is sore, that your head aches, and that nothing looks so good to you as your bed? Perhaps some other member of your family hunts up a thermometer. Your mother gives it a few hard shakes and pops it into your mouth.

If your temperature climbs to over 101 degrees, you may receive a visit from a physician who looks at you, raps your chest, looks down your throat, leaves some pills, and says, "Stay in bed for three days."

When serious illness comes people need the help of a physician. There are times when we would feel lost without expert medical advice. However, many people need more assistance than a doctor can give.

That is where you and I come into the picture—sort of on the fringes. We may not be able to bring a full-fledged cure to some acquaintance who has been ill and does not seem to be gettting back on his feet. But we can brighten up his hospital room a lot.

Jesus made it clear that when we help someone who is sick we are doing his will. In fact, he said that in calling upon such a person we are rendering service to Christ.

Perhaps you have heard your pastor refer to shut-in members of your church, and heard him urging other members to call upon them. Perhaps you have thought, "It would be a good thing to call upon them myself." Then it occurred to you that in facing a sick person you would be tongue-tied and would not know how to make conversation with him.

It is true that a lot of thought and effort and down-right determination are needed before you can make a helpful visit in a sickroom. Why not start planning right now to make such a call? Do some solid thinking about it. Lay out a plan and try to make it work, remembering the words of Jesus, "Truly, I say to you, as you did it to one of the least of these my brethren, you did it to me."

O God of mercy and of love, teach me how to be of service to those who are ill. Give to me a willingness to be used of thee as a messenger of hope and cheerfulness. Help me to say the right word or do the right thing to make someone's load a little lighter. AMEN.

"DON'T FENCE ME IN"

I was in prison and you came to me.

Have you ever been in jail?

Probably spending a night in the county jail is an experience you could well do without. Perhaps sometimes as you have passed a prison you have had a queer feeling. Maybe you have wondered whether by some twist of fate you might some day find yourself under lock and key. Then you pushed such an absurd thought out of your mind.

How do you feel about people who are sent to prison? "Well," you might say about some person who is locked up, "prison was just what he deserved; after all he broke the law." This is the attitude of many people toward those who are put behind bars. But it is not the attitude of Jesus. He put himself in a prisoner's place, and said plainly that his followers should visit those who are in prison.

"Now wait a minute," you may say. "I'm willing to be kind to good, honest people. I'm glad to give a little food to someone who is hungry. I'm pleased to do my share in buying clothes for a poor friend. But this business of going to jail to visit some fellow who is in trouble with the law, well now, that's asking too much."

All of which goes to show that our kindness goes just so far, but no further. When Jesus encouraged his disciples to visit those who are in prison, he was saying quite plainly that we should never put a boundary on our kindness. We should never let our goodness be fenced in. We must never keep our good words and gracious deeds just for our respectable circle of friends.

Some people's kindness is like a meteor. It shoots brilliantly across the sky. Other people's goodness is like a star. It is a steady kind of goodness and doesn't burn its way out in one blazing streak across the sky.

Be like the star and keep your good will burning steadily for all people who are lonely, hungry, in need— yes, and for those, too, who seem to be placed beyond the reach of human kindness. Let the light of friendship know no boundaries—not even prison bars.

Father in heaven, I thank thee that thy love reaches out to the best and worst of men. Teach me never to put a limit on the good will that I should have for all my acquaintances. May that good will and service be ever available to all thy children. AMEN.

LOVE

I CORINTHIANS 13:4-13

Love is patient and kind; love is not jealous or boastful; it is not arrogant or rude. Love does not insist on its own way; it is not irritable or resentful; it does not rejoice at wrong, but rejoices in the right. Love bears all things, believes all things, hopes all things, endures all things.

Love never ends; as for prophecy, it will pass away; as for tongues, they will cease; as for knowledge, it will pass away. For our knowledge is imperfect and our prophecy is imperfect; but when the perfect comes, the imperfect will pass away. When I was a child, I spoke like a child, I thought like a child, I reasoned like a child; when I became a man, I gave up childish ways. For now we see in a mirror dimly, but then face to face. Now I know in part; then I shall understand fully, even as I have been fully understood. So faith, hope, love abide, these three; but the greatest of these is love.

THE ANGRY TREE

Love is patient.

In Idaho there grows a tree which is the wonder of the plant world. It is only eight feet in height when it is full grown. When night comes it coils its leaves together and curls its twigs into shapes like pigtails. If touched after it has settled itself for its "night's sleep," it will flutter as if agitated or impatient with the disturbance. The oftener it is molested the more vigorously the branches will shake. Finally, if the shaking continues, the tree gives off a sickening odor sufficient to inflict a headache on the disturber. This freak of nature is called the "angry tree."

Some of us do no not need much of a shaking to make us throw off words of anger and disgusted glances. We may be people with a pretty low boiling point. We get ruffled quickly and show our impatience.

But Paul tells us how the Christian acts when he has the right kind of good will in his heart. If we have that good will we can "take it." When sly digs and unpleasant words come our way we shall be patient. We shall remember One who was put to death on a cross. We shall think with wonder how when he was reviled, and spat upon, and scourged, and crucified, he said, "Father, forgive them."

This very day he is able to give us the good will to endure without complaint the disagreeable actions and insulting words of others. Let us ask God to give us a full measure of good will.

Dear Father, if things go wrong today, keep me calm in spirit. Save me from chafing at delays, and teach me how, with the help of Christ, I may keep back words of anger and of ill will. In the name of Christ. AMEN.

A SCHOOL FOR KINDNESS

Love is . . . kind.

Have you heard of the school of kindness? It is a strange place. Once a visitor to the school saw a girl, her eyes covered with a bandage, being led carefully between rows of flowers. Her guide directed her every step as she walked through the garden. A teacher told the visitor that the blindfolded girl was not really blind. "This is only her blind day."

A boy in the same school was on crutches. He was not really lame, but this was his lame day.

In the course of a term each pupil has a blind day, a lame day, a deaf day, and a speechless day. This means that help must be given to those who are "in need for a day." The experience of being blind, or lame, or deaf for a day is valuable to those who give help and to those who receive it.

Perhaps your father or mother has scolded you for not eating dinner, saying to you, "You ought to go hungry for just one day and you would appreciate good food." It might do everyone a world of good to attend a school of kindness. Then we would stop talking about kindness and become kind. For in such a school we would learn the significance of kindness.

Great understanding is needed if one is to be truly kind. There is an art to kindness. Study and planning should go into the matter. Kindness is more than simply being good-natured with your friends. There are many people with kind hearts who do not have the foggiest notion of how to do kind things kindly. They mean to say gracious things, but they do not study how to express themselves.

In your youth fellowship there may be another young Christian who needs your assistance. Do you know how to speak the word, or perform the deed, which will bring a blessing to that friend?

O God, help me to see with a clearer eye the troubles of my friends. Guide me in such a way that I shall speak the word or perform the deed which will give just the right lift to somebody's burden. AMEN.

SLAYING THE GREEN-EYED MONSTER

Love is not jealous.

The other day a teen-age girl committed murder. Besides the young girl who was her victim, the lives of several innocent people were blighted. Jackie, who committed the murder, is not going to face a trial in a courtroom. The weapon she used has not been found, for she did not perform the crime with a switch knife or a revolver. Her weapon was a morsel of gossip which she maliciously passed about among several of her acquaintances.

Why did Jackie spread a slander which did so much harm? Simply because she was jealous. She harbored hatred in her heart for a rival. The girl whom she hurt had been her competitor in classroom and in youth fellowship. Jackie had lost out in several contests, and in her jealousy she set out to "get even."

Sometimes we are jealous because our friends have better clothes than we have, or perhaps they have twice as much spending money. Then, too, we get envious when other people's talents outshine ours.

Also, a person who is very popular may arouse jealousy within us. There are some people who have winsome, outgoing personalities. They seem to attract friends just as a magnet draws iron filings. When we see such a popular person surrounded by friends we may feel twinges of jealousy.

Sometimes jealousy is found in churches and youth groups. It is in such places because even Christian people too often center their attention upon themselves. It is hard to cut out of our hearts the desire to be first and the love of glory which are a part of our self-interest. If love has its way in our lives these things will be driven out. Christian love will help us to put aside hurt feelings when an acquaintance goes ahead of us. Christian love will keep us from envying the person who gets to the top of the ladder of success while we stand at the bottom steadying it for him.

O God our father, I thank thee for the talents and abilities which are mine—even though they seem few in number and small in size. Help me to make the most of my gifts without envying others who have more. Guide me into paths of great usefulness to thee. AMEN.

DON'T BE A SELF-ADVERTISER

Love is not . . . boastful

Even a little pat on the back can make the chest stick out. For some people even a brief word of praise will cause them to swell up to twice their normal size. The result—sometimes you see a chap whose hatband is about as large as his belt.

When some young people do not receive the praise they think they deserve, they proceed to praise themselves. A very unpleasant process to behold. You can usually spot a praise-hungry hound; he always has a long tale, and his mouth is always open. He is forever boasting and bragging, and is a thoroughly unpopular fellow.

Why do people brag anyhow? Some brag because they feel very small inside and seek to bolster their feelings of weakness by telling every passer-by that really they are VIP's. The sound of their own voices singing praises to themselves charms away the low opinion they have of themselves—for a time at least.

Paul says that love does not indulge in chest-beating or bragging. The Christian does not need to hang out a neon sign advertising his many abilities, conquests, and accomplishments. The Christian is not so interested in himself as he is interested in serving God and his neighbor. His soul is not so desperately athirst for acknowledgment or recognition.

Love seeks to serve others. This is another way of saying that it does not boast or brag. Love forgets itself and goes out to those who are in trouble. And it will go to the "other side of the railroad tracks" to do it. It will stoop to the very humblest service and expect no flags to be raised in its honor.

Glance for a moment in the direction of one who is our Saviour and Lord. To him belong all our praises and honor, and yet see him at the Last Supper stooping to the lowly task of washing his disciples' feet. Think of it!

How could he do it? Because he loved his followers in life and even unto death. Love serves; it does not boast.

O God, teach me to forget myself, my importance, my rights, my achievements. Guide me into lowly paths of service. In that service may I find freedom from self-seeking. AMEN.

WHEN YOU MISS THE BOAT

Love does not rejoice at wrong, but rejoices in the right.

One day before breakfast a boy was reading the morning newspaper. Usually when he picked up the paper he turned first to the "funnies." This morning he was running his eye down the list of the names of his classmates who had made the honor roll. He knew he had missed the honor for this quarter, but somehow he could not resist the impulse to see the names of his friends whose grades were above eighty-five.

It hurt a little to see the names of so many of his friends who had won recognition. It did give some consolation to note the absence of one of his rivals from the list. "Well, if I didn't make it, neither did he," he said aloud.

Does failure on the part of your acquaintances sometimes give you a good feeling. You say, "Of course not." Are you sure? Really sure? If we were absolutely frank would we not admit that it builds up our own egos to see someone else fail where we, too, have failed?

We live in a country where competition is keen. Rivalry among high-school students is high in class-room, in youth groups, and in trying to make a team. Let us say that you have your heart set upon a class office. When the election comes you fall short. Your popularity quotient was high, but not high enough when the ballots were all counted. In a word, you missed the honor you coveted. Perhaps you did all you could to win and still missed it.

Then comes the acid test of whether you are a genuine Christian. If you do not achieve your dream does it make you happy to see others fall short of their aspirations? Or are you such a mature Christian that you can be glad when another succeeds where you failed? Paul says clearly that Christian love is never glad when others fail, but is ready to rejoice when good things happen to them. Instead of growling have you learned to be happy at the successes of others?

Father in heaven, teach me how to be a good loser. Help me to have the right spirit in my heart when I do not achieve all my dreams. Grant unto me such a victory over myself that others may see in me the triumph of Christian love. AMEN.

EXPECT THE BEST—YOU MAY GET IT

Love . . . believes all things.

Benjamin Franklin's mother-in-law did not think very much of him. In fact, she hesitated to let her daughter marry him. She said he could never make a living as a printer because there were already two printers in the country; surely a third one could not support himself and a wife!

Horace Greeley's relatives did not believe the best about him. One day he absent-mindedly tried to yoke the "off" ox on the "near" side. His father said, "That boy will never get anywhere in the world. He won't know enough to come in when it rains." Such an encouraging remark showed what great expectations Horace's father had for him.

When Thomas Edison was in the first grade his teacher put the worst possible construction on his abilities when she suggested that he be taken out of school because, in her words, he was "too stupid to learn."

Are you sometimes distrustful of your friends? Are you sometimes suspcious of them? Christian love will go to almost any length to believe in right motives and good intentions of others.

It is important that we believe the best about our acquaintances, even when they injure and wound; or even when they take a wrong turn and wind up in real trouble? Love would give them a second chance. That is what God does. He seeks to change a sinful life into one of beauty. That was the mission of Christ to earth— to make men into the godly persons he knew they could become.

A lady once showed a valuable handkerchief to a painter, saying that she had intended it as a gift to a friend. In one corner of the handkerchief was a drop of ink which spoiled its beauty. The painter asked for it, and after a couple of days he returned it to her, and she found that he had transformed the stain into a lovely design. Lives which are stained with wrongdoing can become beautiful when touched by the hand of Christ our Saviour.

For Christ believes in us. He knows that the stained lives of people can be changed and made clean. If Christ so believes in us, then we, as Christians, should look at others through the eyes of love, knowing that they possess possibilities hidden from all eyes but his.

Gracious God, keep me from bitter criticism of my friends and acquaintances, not asking nor expecting more of them than I expect of myself. Sharpen my vision so that I may see the best in all people. AMEN.

NO ONE IS HOPELESS

Love . . . hopes all things.

Robert Louis Stevenson, who wrote *Treasure Island* and *Kidnapped,* once said that he believed in the ultimate decency of things. And then he added, "If I woke in hell, I should still believe in it." Stevenson was a man of hope.

In these days hope is not always easy to come by. We wonder whether mankind, with his intercontinental ballistic missiles, his rockets, and his atomic bombs, is getting ready for full-dress suicide. When we get too gloomy about the future we would do well to remember Stevenson's words of hope. If he—a man dying of tuberculosis—could keep hopeful, we should not lose faith in the "ultimate decency of things."

Do you believe in the ultimate decency of *people?* Of course it is an easy matter to have high hopes for some people. At least a few of our friends show signs of achieving great things. Here is a high-school senior who studies faithfully, has a winsome personality, is serious about every responsibility, respects his parents, is loyal to his church. Here is a girl who never has strayed two blocks from her mother's raised eyebrows. It is easy to hope great things of such young people.

But what about the boy or girl who just can't seem to stay on even keel? They spend their days getting into and out of trouble. Well, a good father and mother always wait hopefully for a change to come in their son's life if he has not played the man. They wait expectantly for his reformation, just as the father waited expectantly for the return of the prodigal son in Jesus' famous story. The love of a good father and mother will never throw in the towel and cry, "Hopeless."

Do you have acquaintances in your youth fellowship who are "difficult"? Perhaps one of them refuses to co-operate. He "crabs" at the leader's suggestions. He gripes at the programs. Or worse still he drifts away from the church and heads for real trouble. How should he be treated? You will not cut him out of your interest and cease to be his friend. Neither will you congratulate yourself by saying, "I'm not like him; I know how to behave myself and stay out of trouble." If you have Christian love in your heart, you will go on hoping that he may change. For love hopes all things.

Eternal God, I thank thee for thy great patience. I acknowledge that I do not always deserve thy love by the quality of my life. As thou hast not abandoned me, may I never abandon my friends. Help me to pray for them, work for them, and always hope the best for them. AMEN.

STEADFAST THROUGH THE YEARS

So faith, hope, love abide, these three; but the greatest of these is love.

Has some honor come to you lately? Perhaps you wrote an article for your school paper. How eagerly you read your copy when it came out! It made you feel pretty good to see your name signed to something which burst into print. Your friends congratulated you, and you were elated. An honor had come to you.

But did you notice how short-lived was that honor? For a while a little glory stirred your flag. But soon a new issue of the paper appeared and somebody else was getting the glory. Glory does not last.

Or possibly you were elected to a class office or to the presidency of your youth fellowship. You did your job well as an official and people seemed to appreciate your good work. The following year someone else was elected and your past services were forgotten. Appreciation often does not last.

A great philosopher once said, "This, too, shall pass away." When you read the writings of this great thinker, whose name was Marcus Aurelius, you get the impression that he thought there is nothing permanent in this world.

Well, everybody wishes to believe there *is* something that is enduring, and imperishable. Paul was sure that some things never die. He said, "So faith, hope, love abide." Now we have rocklike values upon which to build our lives—faith, hope, and love. When we live close to God, seeking every day to carry out his holy will, he will deepen and strengthen our faith. That faith will endure forever.

Hope is another foundation which cannot be shaken if we walk in the path that Christ has chosen for us. Even in these days of world crisis hope will endure for every Christian. And love will endure. The love of God, which is as old as the sun and moon and stars, will never fail. God himself is love and the everlasting God remains the same.

Almighty Father, in moments of doubt and disappointment help me to learn how to depend upon thee. When other people seem to fail me and nothing seems to be enduring, teach me to listen to thee who art the everlasting one. AMEN.

#956